LEVEL 7 Supplemental

EXAM SERIES ANSWERS

By Glory St. Germain ARCT RMT MYCC UMTC &
Shelagh McKibbon-U'Ren RMT UMTC

ULTIMATE
MUSIC THEORY

GSG MUSIC

Enriching Lives Through Music Education

ISBN: 978-1-990358-16-6

The Ultimate Music Theory™ Program

Enriching Lives Through Music Education

The Ultimate Music Theory™ Workbooks & Answer Books Program includes:

UMT Rudiments Workbooks for Prep 1, Prep 2, Basic, Intermediate, Advanced & Complete
UMT Exam Series (Set #1 & Set #2) for Preparatory, Basic, Intermediate & Advanced

Supplemental Workbooks for PREP LEVEL, LEVELS 1 - 8 & COMPLETE LEVEL
UMT Supplemental Exam Series for LEVEL 5, LEVEL 6, LEVEL 7 & LEVEL 8

The Ultimate Music Theory Program is the *Way to Score Success* as UMT helps students prepare for nationally recognized theory examinations including the Royal Conservatory of Music.

Library and Archives Canada Cataloguing in Publication. UMT Workbooks & Exam Series /Glory St. Germain & Shelagh McKibbon-U'Ren. Respect Copyright. All rights reserved. GlorylandPublishing.com

Ultimate Music Theory Rudiments Exam Series

GP - EPS1	ISBN: 978-1-927641-00-2	Preparatory Rudiments Exams Set #1
GP - EPS1A	ISBN: 978-1-927641-08-8	Preparatory Exams Answers Set #1
GP - EPS2	ISBN: 978-1-927641-01-9	Preparatory Rudiments Exams Set #2
GP - EPS2A	ISBN: 978-1-927641-09-5	Preparatory Exams Answers Set #2
GP - EBS1	ISBN: 978-1-927641-02-6	Basic Rudiments Exams Set #1
GP - EBS1A	ISBN: 978-1-927641-10-1	Basic Exams Answers Set #1
GP - EBS2	ISBN: 978-1-927641-03-3	Basic Rudiments Exams Set #2
GP - EBS2A	ISBN: 978-1-927641-11-8	Basic Exams Answers Set #2
GP - EIS1	ISBN: 978-1-927641-04-0	Intermediate Rudiments Exams Set #1
GP - EIS1A	ISBN: 978-1-927641-12-5	Intermediate Exams Answers Set #1
GP - EIS2	ISBN: 978-1-927641-05-7	Intermediate Rudiments Exams Set #2
GP - EIS2A	ISBN: 978-1-927641-13-2	Intermediate Exams Answers Set #2
GP - EAS1	ISBN: 978-1-927641-06-4	Advanced Rudiments Exams Set #1
GP - EAS1A	ISBN: 978-1-927641-14-9	Advanced Exams Answers Set #1
GP - EAS2	ISBN: 978-1-927641-07-1	Advanced Rudiments Exams Set #2
GP - EAS2A	ISBN: 978-1-927641-15-6	Advanced Exams Answers Set #2

Ultimate Music Theory Supplemental Exam Series

GP-L5E	ISBN: 978-1-990358-11-1	LEVEL 5 Exams
GP-L5EA	ISBN: 978-1-990358-12-8	LEVEL 5 Exams Answers
GP-L6E	ISBN: 978-1-990358-13-5	LEVEL 6 Exams
GP-L6EA	ISBN: 978-1-990358-14-2	LEVEL 6 Exams Answers
GP-L7E	ISBN: 978-1-990358-15-9	LEVEL 7 Exams
GP-L7EA	ISBN: 978-1-990358-16-6	LEVEL 7 Exams Answers
GP-L8E	ISBN: 978-1-990358-17-3	LEVEL 8 Exams
GP-L8EA	ISBN: 978-1-990358-18-0	LEVEL 8 Exams Answers

Go to UltimateMusicTheory.com and check out the FREE Resources

Ultimate Music Theory FREE RESOURCES created just for you!

Ultimate Music Theory
LEVEL 7 Supplemental Exams

Table of Contents

Ultimate Music Theory: *The Way to Score Success!*

The 2016 RCM Theory Syllabus has added the Level 7 Theory Examination, to be completed after the Level 6 Theory Exam (formerly the Intermediate Rudiments Exam), and covers:

♫ **All Concepts introduced in the Ultimate Music Theory Intermediate Workbook.**
♫ **All New Concepts introduced in the Level 6 Supplemental Workbook PLUS:**
♫ **Pitch and Notation:** Transposition of melodies up **or down** by any interval or to any key.
♫ **Rhythm and Meter:** Double dotted notes and rests.
♫ **Intervals:** All intervals above **or below** a given note within an octave.
♫ **Chords and Harmony**: Triads built on any degree of a Major or minor (harmonic) scale using Functional Chord Symbols and Root/Quality Chord Symbols.
   - Leading-Tone Diminished 7th Chords in minor keys, Root Position only, using Functional Chord Symbols (viiº7) and Root/Quality Chord Symbols (Eº7).
   - Dominant 7th Chords and their inversions, using Functional Chord Symbols and Root/Quality Chord Symbols.
   - Identification **and writing** of Authentic and Half Cadences on a Grand Staff, using Root Position Chords in Major and minor keys, in Keyboard Style.
♫ **Melody and Composition**: Melodic Passing and Neighbor Tones (unaccented only), within a harmonic context of I, IV and V (Major keys) or i, iv and V (minor keys).
   - Composition of a Contrasting Period in a Major Key, given the Antecedent Phrase.
♫ **Form and Analysis**: Application of Functional or Root/Quality Chord Symbols to a melody, using Root Position I, IV and V Chords (Major keys) or i, iv and V Chords (minor keys), maintaining a harmonic rhythm of one chord per measure.
♫ **Musical Terms and Signs**: New Terms and Signs have been added.
♫ **Music History**: Introduction to Musical Styles of the Romantic and Modern Eras. "Overture to A Midsummer Night's Dream"; "Etude in c minor, opus 10, no. 12" ("Revolutionary"); "Petrushka"; "Dripsody"; and "Ko-Ko". (To include Composer, Genre, Performing Forces and Style Traits.)

Circle of Fifths

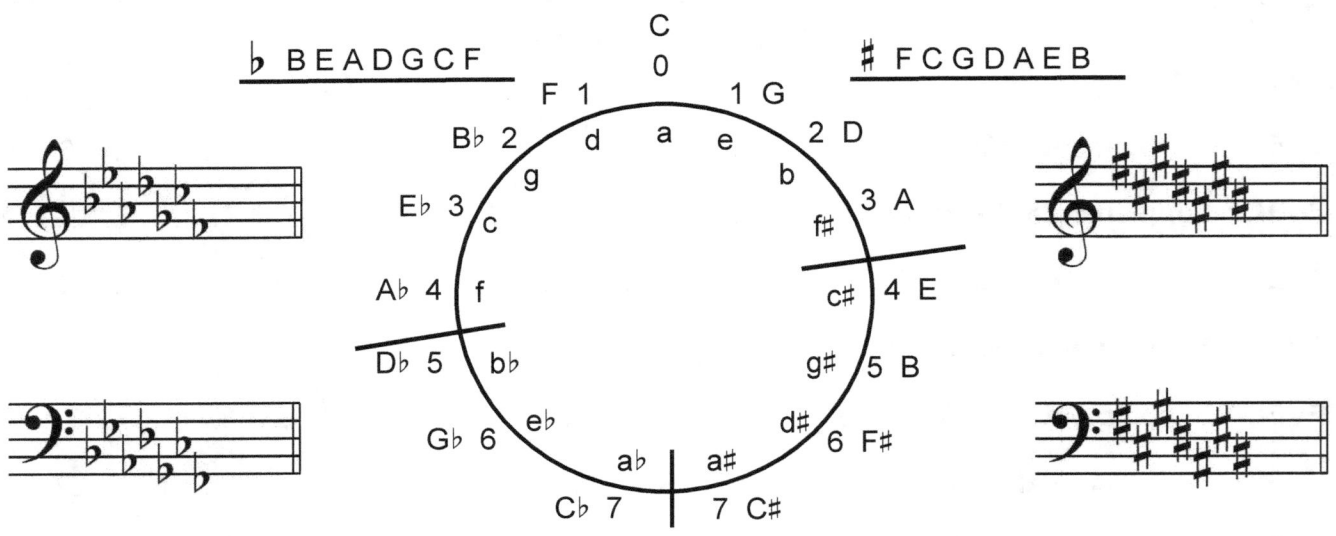

♭ B E A D G C F   ♯ F C G D A E B

C 0
F 1   1 G
B♭ 2   2 D
d   a   e
g   b
E♭ 3   3 A
c   f♯
A♭ 4   f   c♯   4 E
g♯   5 B
D♭ 5   b♭   d♯   6 F♯
G♭ 6   e♭   a♯
a♭
C♭ 7   7 C♯

Key	Chord Root	Quality	Root/Quality	Functional Chord	Inversion Symbols			
E Major	A	Major	A	IV	IV	IV^6	IV$^6_4$	
e minor	A	minor	Am	iv	A	A/C♯	A/E	
e minor	G	Augmented	G+ or Gaug	III+				
E Maj / e min	B	Dominant 7th	B7	V7	V^7	V$^6_5$	V$^4_3$	V$^4_2$
e minor	D♯	diminished	D♯° or D♯dim	vii°	B7	B7/D♯	B7/F♯	B7/A
e minor	D♯	diminished 7th	D♯°7 or D♯dim7	vii°7				

"Irregular Group"	Simple Time	Compound Time
2		2 = 3
3	3 = 2	
4		4 = 3
5	5 = 4	5 = 3 or 5 = 6
6	6 = 4	
7	7 = 4	7 = 3 or 7 = 6

# of Notes: (+ Upper Tonic)	Ti-Do Tip:	Type of Scale:
6 notes	1st interval: Major 2	Major pentatonic
6 notes	1st interval: minor 3	minor pentatonic
7 notes	7 different notes	Whole Tone scale
7 notes	$\hat{4}$ or $\hat{5}$ twice	Blues scale
8 notes	Major or minor (natural, harmonic or melodic)	
9 notes	Alternate HS & WS	Octatonic scale
13 notes	All half steps	Chromatic scale

Melody Writing

Parallel Period: a + a1

Contrasting Period: a + b

Stable Scale Degrees: $\hat{1}$ and $\hat{3}$

Unstable Scale Degrees: $\hat{2}$ and $\hat{7}$

Exam Tip: Copy the UMT Map for LEVEL 7 below. Using a blank piece of paper, write out the UMT Map from memory before beginning each practice exam and the final exam.

Circle of Fifths

♭ BEADGCF   C/O   # FCGDAEB

Key	Chord Root	Quality	Root/Quality	Functional Chord	Inversion Symbols		
E Major	A	Major	A	IV	IV	IV⁶	IV⁶₄
e minor	A	minor	Am	iv	A	A/C♯	A/E
e minor	G	Augmented	G⁺ or Gaug	III⁺			
E Maj / e min	B	Dominant 7ᵗʰ	B7	V7	V⁷	V⁶₅	V⁴₃ V⁴₂
e minor	D♯	diminished	D♯° or D♯dim	vii°	B7	B7/D♯	B7/F♯ B7/A
e minor	D♯	diminished 7ᵗʰ	D♯°7 or D♯dim⁷	vii°7			

"Irregular Group"	Simple Time	Compound Time
⌐2⌐		2 = 3
⌐3⌐	3 = 2	.
⌐4⌐		4 = 3
⌐5⌐	5 = 4	5 = 3 or 5 = 6
⌐6⌐	6 = 4	
⌐7⌐	7 = 4	7 = 3 or 7 = 6

# of Notes: (+ Upper Tonic)	Ti-Do Tip:	Type of Scale:
6 notes	1st interval: Major 2	Major pentatonic
6 notes	1st interval: minor 3	minor pentatonic
7 notes	7 different notes	Whole Tone Scale
7 notes	4̂ or 5̂ twice	Blues scale
8 notes	Major or minor (natural, harmonic or melodic)	
9 notes	Alternate HS & WS	Octatonic scale
13 notes	All half steps	Chromatic scale

Melody Writing

Parallel Period: a + a1

Contrasting Period: a + b

Stable Scale Degrees: 1̂ and 3̂

Unstable Scale Degrees: 2̂ and 7̂

Ultimate Music Theory
LEVEL 7 Supplemental Exam #1

Total Score: _____
100

The Ultimate Music Theory™ Intermediate Rudiments Workbook, LEVELS 6 & 7 Supplemental Workbooks, Intermediate Rudiments Exam Series and Level 7 Supplemental Exams prepare students for successful completion of the Royal Conservatory of Music Level 7 Theory Examination.

1. Write the following Solid (Blocked) Triads or Chords. Use whole notes. Use a Key Signature and any necessary accidentals. Write the Root/Quality Chord Symbol above and the Functional Chord Symbol below.

10
a) The Supertonic Triad of D Major, in second inversion.
b) The Subdominant Triad of d minor, harmonic form, in first inversion.
c) The Leading Tone Triad of e flat minor, harmonic form, in root position.
d) The Mediant Triad of A Major, in second inversion.
e) The Dominant Seventh Chord of E Major, in third inversion.

2. Write the following harmonic interval below each of the given notes. Use whole notes.

10

| Perfect 8 | Augmented 6 | Major 7 | minor 3 | diminished 4 |

| Major 3 | Perfect 4 | Major 2 | minor 7 | Augmented 5 |

3. a) Name the key of this melody.
    b) Compose a four-measure Answer phrase to create a **Contrasting** Period. End on a stable scale degree. (There will be more than one correct answer.)
    c) Draw a phrase mark over the Question (Antecedent) phrase and over the contrasting Answer (Consequent) phrase.
    d) Label the type of cadence (Authentic or Half) at the end of each phrase.

___
10

Key: G Major   Cadence: Half

                                                  Cadence: Authentic

4.   Match each musical term or sign with the English definition. (Not all definitions will be used.)

Term		Definition
agitato	c	a) resolute
giocoso	i	b) above
martellato	f	c) agitated
morendo	l	d) two octaves higher
risoluto	a	e) sad
semplice	j	f) strongly accented, hammered
sopra	b	g) lively
tutti	k	h) one octave higher
vivo	g	i) humorous, jocose
dolente	e	j) simple
quindicesima alta, 15ma	d	k) a passage for the ensemble
		l) dying, fading away

___
10

5.   Answer the following questions.

a) Name the composer of "Dripsody".

10   Hugh LeCaine

b) Name the composer of the "Overture to A Midsummer Night's Dream".

Mendelssohn

c) Name the composer of "Ko-Ko".

Duke Ellington

d) Name the composer of "Petrushka".

Stravinsky

e) Name the composer of "Etude in c minor, opus 10, number 12".

Chopin

f) Name the type of instrumental music with a descriptive title based on a literary idea.

Program Music

g) Name the type of music that is a single-movement concert piece for an orchestra.

Concert Overture

h) Name the musical structure used in Jazz that is based upon the I, IV and V chords.

Twelve Bar Blues

i) Name the genre of music that is produced or modified by devices such as synthesizers.

Electronic Music

j) Name the genre of music that is non-verbal storytelling through choreography performed to music.

Ballet

6. Add rests below the brackets to complete each of the following measures.

7. The following melody is in the key of B flat Major.

a) Transpose the given melody down a Perfect fourth in the same clef. Use the correct Key Signature. Name the new key.

Key: _F Major_

b) Transpose the given melody up into the key of D Major in the same clef. Name the interval of transposition.

Interval of Transposition: _Major 3_

8. For each of the following Seventh Chords:

    a) Name the key.
    b) Label the chord using a Functional Chord Symbol.

10

Key: a) a#minor b) d minor c) C Major d) A♭Major e) e minor

Functional
Chord Symbol: a) V^6_5 b) vii^{o7} c) V^4_2 d) V^6_5 e) V^7

9. For each of the following excerpts:

    a) Name the key.
    b) Write the Root/Quality Chord Symbol (root position) implied by the melody on the line above.
    c) Write the Functional Chord Symbol (root position) implied by the melody on the line below.
    10 d) Circle and label any passing tones as pt. Circle and label any neighbor tones as nt.

Root/Quality
Chord Symbol: E♭m   A♭m   E♭m   B♭

Key: e♭ minor

Functional
Chord Symbol: i   iv   i   V

Root/Quality
Chord Symbol: D   A   E   A

Key: A Major

Functional
Chord Symbol: IV   I   V   I

10. Analyze this excerpt from Julianne Warkentin's arrangement of "King Wenceslas Stomp" by answering the questions below.

a) For the triad at letter **A**, identify: Root: _F_   Quality: _Major_   Position: _1st inv_

b) For the triad at letter **B**, identify: Root: _G_   Quality: _minor_   Position: _1st inv_

c) Explain the term at letter **C**. _ritardando - slowing down gradually_

d) Explain the sign at letter **D**. _pedal marking_

e) Explain the term at letter **E**. _return to the original tempo_

f) Identify the interval at letter **F**. _dim 5_.   Identify the interval at letter **G**. _Per 4_.

g) Explain the sign at letter **H**. _held, sustained, a stressed note._

h) Explain the sign at letter **I**. _staccato - sharply detached_

i) Explain the sign at letter **J**. _play one octave below the written pitch_

j) Add the missing rests at letter **K**.

1. For each of the following excerpts:

    a) Name the key.
    ___ b) Write the Root/Quality Chord Symbol (root position) implied by the melody on the line above.
    10 c) Write the Functional Chord Symbol (root position) implied by the melody on the line below.
    d) Circle and label any passing tones as pt. Circle and label any neighbor tones as nt.

Root/Quality
Chord Symbol: **Cm**   **Fm**   **G**   **Cm**

Key: **C minor**

Functional
Chord Symbol: **i**   **iv**   **V**   **i**

Root/Quality
Chord Symbol: **F#**   **B**   **F#**   **C#**

Key: **F# Major**

Functional
Chord Symbol: **I**   **IV**   **I**   **V**

2. Write one note or one rest that equals the total value of the notes or rests when added together.

Ultimate Music Theory
LEVEL 7 Supplemental Exam #2

3. a) Write the following melodic interval below each of the given notes. Use whole notes.

10

        minor 6   Major 2   Augmented 5   Perfect 4   diminished 3

b) Invert the above intervals in the same clef. Name the inversions.

    Maj 3   min 7   dim 4   Per 5   Aug 6

4. Add the correct Time Signature below each bracket to complete the following rhythms.

10

5. Write the following Solid (Blocked) Chords. Use whole notes. Use a Key Signature and any necessary accidentals. Write the Root/Quality Chord Symbol above and the Functional Chord Symbol below.

10 a) The Dominant Seventh Chord of b flat minor in first inversion.
    b) The Dominant Seventh Chord of B flat Major in third inversion.
    c) The Leading-Tone Diminished Seventh Chord of e minor in root position.
    d) The Dominant Seventh Chord of g sharp minor in second inversion.
    e) The Leading-Tone Diminished Seventh Chord of f minor in root position.

Root/Quality Chord Symbol: a) F^7/A b) F^7/E^b c) $D^{\#o7}$ d) $D^{\#7}/A^\#$ e) E^{o7}

Functional Chord Symbol: a) V^6_5 b) V^4_2 c) vii^{o7} d) V^4_3 e) vii^{o7}

6. Circle TRUE or FALSE for each of the following statements.

   a) TRUE or (FALSE) The Genre of Mendelssohn's A Midsummer Night's Dream is an Aria.

10 b) (TRUE) or FALSE: The Form used in A Midsummer Night's Dream is Sonata Form.

   c) (TRUE) or FALSE: Chopin's Étude Opus 10, No 12 is known as the Revolutionary Étude.

   d) (TRUE) or FALSE: The Form of Chopin's Étude Op. 10, No. 12 is Ternary Form (ABA1).

   e) (TRUE) or FALSE: The Genre of Stravinsky's Petrushka is a Ballet.

   f) TRUE or (FALSE) The Performing Forces of Petrushka are solo violin and piano.

   g) (TRUE) or FALSE: The Genre of Le Caine's Dripsody is Electronic Music.

   h) (TRUE) or FALSE: Le Caine used a Special Purpose Tape Recorder to compose Dripsody.

   i) (TRUE) or FALSE: The Genre of Duke Ellington's Ko-Ko is Jazz for Big Band.

   j) (TRUE) or FALSE: The Form (or Musical Structure) of Ko-Ko is 12 Bar Blues.

7. Following the instructions, write the scales ascending and descending. Use whole notes.

a) The Chromatic scale starting on A flat. Use accidentals. Use any standard notation.

10

b) The Whole Tone scale starting on E. Use accidentals. Use any standard notation.
(Also acceptable: E Gb Ab Bb C D E)

c) The Parallel minor scale, melodic form, of F Sharp Major. Use accidentals.

d) The Enharmonic Tonic minor scale, natural form, of A flat Major. Use a Key Signature.

e) The Enharmonic Relative Major scale of b flat minor. Use a Key Signature.

8. For each of the following melodies:

    a) Name the key of the melody.
    b) Mark the two four-measure phrases with a slur.
    c) Name the type of each Cadence (Authentic or Half).
    d) Circle the correct answer for each question.

$\dfrac{}{10}$

Melody #1:

Key: __A♭ Major__   Cadence: __Half__

Cadence: __Authentic__

    i) Melody #1 is an example of: a Parallel Period   or   (a Contrasting Period.)

Melody #2:

Key: __D Major__   Cadence: __Half__

Cadence: __Authentic__

    ii) Melody #2 is an example of: (a Parallel Period)   or   a Contrasting Period.

9. a) Provide the name of the new key for each of the following transpositions.

10

Original Key	Interval of Transposition	New Key
D flat Major	Down a diminished fifth	G Major
g sharp minor	Up a Perfect fourth	c# minor
E Major	Up a minor second	F Major
f minor	Down a diminished sixth	a# minor
G flat Major	Up an Augmented fourth	C Major
a minor	Down a minor third	f# minor
e minor	Up a Perfect fifth	b minor
D Major	Down a Major third	B♭ Major
e flat minor	Down a minor seventh	f minor
F Major	Up a Major sixth	D Major

b) Provide the interval (and direction) of transposition for the following pairs of keys.

Original Key	New Key	Interval of Transposition
C Major	Up to D Major	Up a Major 2
E flat Major	Up to B Major	Up an Augmented 5
f sharp minor	Down to d sharp minor	Down a Minor 3
A flat Major	Down to B flat Major	Down a minor 7
C flat Major	Up to A Major	Up an Augmented 6
a sharp minor	Up to f minor	Up a diminished 6
g minor	Down to e flat minor	Down a Major 3
F sharp Major	Up to A flat Major	Up a diminished 3
G Major	Down to C Major	Down a Perfect 5
c minor	Up to f sharp minor	Up an Augmented 4

10. Analyze this excerpt from Variation II of Mozart's 12 Variations on "Ah, Vous Dirai-Je, Maman" by answering the questions below.

a) Name the key of this excerpt. __C Major__

b) Circle a recurrence of the notes (melodic and rhythmic) at letter **A**.

c) For the triad at letter **B**, identify: Root: __F__ Quality: __Major__ Position: __2nd inv__

d) The triad at letter **B** is the: ☐ Tonic Triad ☒ Subdominant Triad ☐ Dominant Triad.

e) For the triad at letter **C**, identify: Root: __E__ Quality: __diminished__ Position: __2nd inv__

f) Identify the interval at letter **D**. __Maj 2__. Identify the interval at letter **E**. __min 2__.

g) This excerpt begins on Measure 65. Add the Measure Number in the box at letter **F**.

h) Circle an example of a Whole Step (Whole Tone). Label it as "WS".

i) Circle an example of a Diatonic Half Step (Diatonic Semitone). Label it as "DH".

j) In this excerpt: Identify the number of ties. __8__ Identify the number of slurs. __0__

1. For the following melody:

   a) Name the key.
   b) Above the staff, write the Root/Quality Chord Symbol (in root position) outlined by the notes in each measure.
   c) Below the staff, write the Functional Chord Symbol (in root position) outlined by the notes in each measure.
   d) Circle and label any passing tones as pt. Circle and label any neighbor tones as nt.

2. Add rests below the brackets to complete each of the following measures.

Ultimate Music Theory
LEVEL 7 Supplemental Exam #3

3. For each of the following Dominant Seventh or Leading-Tone Diminished Seventh Chords:

    a) Name the key.

    ___
    10
    b) Write the Root/Quality Chord Symbol above and the Functional Chord Symbol below.

Root/Quality
Chord Symbol:

Key: B Major   b minor   c minor   Db Major   f# minor

Functional
Chord Symbol: V^6_5 V^4_2 vii^{o7} V^4_2 V^7

4. Write the following Solid (Blocked) Triads or Chords (in close position). Use a Key Signature and accidentals as needed. Use whole notes.

Key: C Major   b minor   c# minor   Bb Major   d minor

Functional
Chord Symbol: iii^6_4 $III+^6$ vii^o V^4_3 V^6_5

Root/Quality
Chord Symbol: G#o/B   D7/F#   Eb+   Cm/G   D#o7

Key: a minor   G Major   c minor   Ab Major   e minor

5. The following melody is in the key of F Sharp Major.

a) Transpose the given melody down an Augmented Third in the same clef. Use the correct Key Signature. Name the new key.

10

Key: __D♭ Major__

b) Transpose the given melody up into the key of B flat Major in the same clef. Name the interval of transposition.

Interval of Transposition: __Up a diminished 4__

6. Name the following intervals.

10

Per 4   Maj 3   min 6   dim 3   dim 8

Maj 7   Aug 1   min 2   dim 5   Maj 6

7. a) Name the key.
    b) Write a Cadence in Keyboard Style below the bracketed notes.
    c) Label the chords using Functional Chord Symbols.
    d) Name the type of Cadence (Authentic or Half).

___
10

Key: __E♭ Major__   IV   V   V   I

Cadence: __Half__   Cadence: __Authentic__
(IV A♭ C E♭   V B♭ D F)   (V B♭ D F   I E♭ G B♭)

Key: __b minor__   i   V   V   i

Cadence: __Half__   Cadence: __Authentic__
(i B D F♯   V F♯ A♯ C♯)   (V F♯ A♯ C♯   i B D F♯)

8. Add bar lines to complete each of the following rhythms.

___
10

9. a) Name the following scales as Whole Tone, Octatonic, Major Pentatonic, minor Pentatonic or Blues.

$\overline{10}$ i) ___Blues___

ii) ___Whole Tone___

iii) ___Octatonic___

iv) ___minor Pentatonic___

v) ___Major Pentatonic___

vi) ___Blues___

b) Write the Chromatic scale starting on B flat, ascending and descending. Use a Key Signature. Use any standard notation. Use whole notes.

(one possible answer)

c) Write the Chromatic scale starting on D, ascending and descending. Use accidentals. Use any standard notation. Use whole notes.

(one possible answer)

10. Analyze this excerpt from Variation XI of Mozart's 12 Variations on "Ah, Vous Dirai-Je, Maman" by answering the questions below.

Adagio

a) Name the key of this excerpt. <u>C Major</u>

b) Explain the sign at letter **A**. <u>repeat the music within the double bar lines</u>

c) Circle a recurrence of the notes (melodic and rhythmic) at letter **B** written one octave lower.

d) Explain the sign at letter **C**. <u>fp fortepiano - loud then suddenly soft</u>

e) Identify the interval at letter **D**. <u>Maj 2</u>. Identify the interval at letter **E**. <u>dim 3</u>

f) Add the correct rest at letter **F**. Name the type of rest. <u>eighth rest</u>

g) Add the correct rest at letter **G**. Name the type of rest. <u>sixteenth rest</u>

h) For the triad at letter **H**, identify: Root: <u>B</u> Quality: <u>diminished</u> Position: <u>2nd inv</u>

i) For the triad at letter **I**, identify: Root: <u>C</u> Quality: <u>Major</u> Position: <u>2nd inv</u>

j) Identify the cadence at letter **J**: <u>Authentic (V^7 I)</u>

Ultimate Music Theory
LEVEL 7 Supplemental Exam #4

Total Score: _____
/ 100

1. For each of the following Seventh Chords:

   a) Name the key.
___ b) Write the Root/Quality Chord Symbol above each Chord.
10 c) Write the Functional Chord Symbol below each Chord.

Root/Quality
Chord Symbol: G^7 E^7/B A^7/G D^{o7} $G^{\#7}/D^{\#}$

Key: C Major   A Major   d minor   eb minor   c# minor

Functional
Chord Symbol: V^7 V^4_3 V^4_2 vii^{o7} V^4_3

2. For the following melody:

   a) Name the key.
   b) Above the staff, write the Root/Quality Chord Symbol (in root position) outlined by the notes
10   in each measure.
   c) Below the staff, write the Functional Chord Symbol (in root position) outlined by the notes in
   each measure.
   d) Circle and label any passing tones as pt. Circle and label any neighbor tones as nt.

Root/Quality
Chord Symbol: Gm   Cm   Gm   D

Key: g minor

Functional
Chord Symbol: i   iv   i   V

3. a) Write the following harmonic interval below each of the given notes. Use whole notes.

minor 2   Major 7   Augmented 4   diminished 8   Perfect 5

b) Invert the above intervals in the same clef. Name the inversions.

Major 7   minor 2   dim 5   Aug 1   Per 4

4. a) Name the key.
   b) Write a Cadence in Keyboard Style below the bracketed notes.
   c) Label the chords using Functional Chord Symbols.
   d) Name the type of Cadence (Authentic or Half).

Key: C minor   i   V   V   i

Cadence: _____Half_____   Cadence: _Authentic_

Key: B Major   IV   V   V   I

Cadence: _____Half_____   Cadence: _Authentic_

5. Write the term or word that each of the following statements applies to. Use the following terms/words (not all terms/words will be used):

___
10

✓Polytonality   ✓Petrushka Chord   ✓Concert Overture   ✓Modern Era   ✓Romantic Era

✓Program Music   ✓Jazz   Rondo   ✓Nationalism   ✓Étude   ✓Chromaticism   Rubato

a) __Polytonality__ - The use of 2 or more keys sounding simultaneously (at the same time) to create dissonance (tension).

b) __Program Music__ - Instrumental music that is given a descriptive title and is written to suggest images or musical ideas for the listener.

c) __Modern Era__ - The musical period from around 1900 to the present that features innovation, advancement in technology and originality in composition.

d) __Nationalism__ - The use of musical ideas that are identified with a Composer's Country or Region to show patriotism.

e) __Romantic Era__ - The musical period from around 1825 to 1900 that features freedom of expression and personal feelings in music, poetry and art.

f) __Étude__ - French for "study", this type of composition for solo instrument is written to "study" 1 or 2 specific playing techniques.

g) __Concert Overture__ - A single movement piece for orchestra (often in Sonata Form or a Symphonic Poem Form) that tells a story or describes a scene.

h) __Petrushka Chord__ - A Polychord of C Major and F sharp Major (a tritone apart) that creates a dissonant sound used to identify the title character of the Ballet.

i) __Jazz__ - Music that is a mix or fusion of European musical ideas with African-American styles using syncopation, rhythmic pulse and improvisation.

j) __Chromaticism__ - Greek for "color", this is the use of notes that do not belong to the Key or Key Signature in order to add "color" or dissonance to the harmony.

6. Write the following Solid (Blocked) Triads in the Treble Clef using a Key Signature and any necessary accidentals. Use whole notes. Write the Root/Quality Chord Symbol above the triad and the Functional Chord Symbol below.

10 a) The Supertonic Triad of B flat Major in second inversion.
   b) The Submediant Triad of b minor harmonic form in first inversion.
   c) The Leading Tone Triad of E Major in root position.
   d) The Subdominant Triad of c minor harmonic form in second inversion.
   e) The Mediant Triad of A flat Major in first inversion.

Root/Quality
Chord Symbol: a) Cm/G   b) G/B   c) D#°   d) Fm/C   e) Cm/Eb

Functional
Chord Symbol: a) ii⁶₄   b) VI⁶₃   c) vii°   d) iv⁶₄   e) iii⁶₃

7. Match each musical term or sign with the English definition. (Not all definitions will be used.)

Term		Definition
volti subito, v.s.	d	a) hammered, strongly accented
con fuoco	i	b) be silent
simile	k	c) agitated
martellato	a	d) turn the page quickly
risoluto	j	e) sustained
con grazia	h	f) sad, mournful
tacet	b	g) with motion
mesto	f	h) with grace
con moto	g	i) with fire
sostenuto	e	j) resolute
		k) continue in the same manner as has just been indicated

8. Add rests below the brackets to complete each of the following measures.

9. a) Name the key of the following melody.

Key: d minor

b) Rewrite the melody at the same pitch. Use a Key Signature and any necessary accidentals.

c) Transpose the melody down a Major Second in the same clef. Use a Key Signature and any necessary accidentals. Name the new key.

Key: c minor

10. Analyze this excerpt from Chopin's Etude in c sharp minor, Opus 25, number 7 by answering the questions below.

a) Explain the sign at letter **A**. *sf - sforzando - a sudden strong accent of a single note or chord (also written as "sfz)*

b) Identify the interval at letter **B**. *min 2*.   Identify the interval at letter **C**. *Maj 2*.

c) Identify the interval at letter **D**. *Maj 2*.   Identify the interval at letter **E**. *Aug 2*.

d) Explain the sign at letter **F**. *accent - a stressed note*

e) For the triad at letter **G**, identify: Root: *F#*   Quality: *minor*   Position: *2nd inv*

f) Circle a recurrence of the notes (melodic and rhythmic) at letter **H** written one octave higher.

g) For the triad at letter **I**, identify: Root: *A*   Quality: *Major*   Position: *1st inv*

h) Circle an example of a Whole Step (Whole Tone). Label it as "WS".

i) Circle an example of a Diatonic Half Step (Diatonic Semitone). Label it as "DH".

j) In this excerpt: Identify the number of ties. *2*   Identify the number of slurs. *6*

1. For each of the following Seventh Chords:

___ a) Name the key.
10 b) Write the Root/Quality Chord Symbol above each Chord.
c) Write the Functional Chord Symbol below each Chord.

Root/Quality
Chord Symbol: C⁷/E   A⁷/G   A#⁷   C⁷/G   E#⁰⁷

Key: F Major   D Major   d# minor   f minor   f# minor

Functional
Chord Symbol: V⁶₅   V⁴₂   V⁷   V⁴₃   vii⁰⁷

2. a) Name the key of this melody.
   b) Compose a four-measure Answer phrase to create a **Contrasting** Period. End on a stable scale degree. (There will be more than one correct answer.)
   c) Draw a phrase mark over the Question (Antecedent) phrase and over the contrasting Answer
10   (Consequent) phrase.
   d) Label the type of cadence (Authentic or Half) at the end of each phrase.

Key: C# Major   Cadence: Half

(one possible answer)   Cadence: Authentic

3. Add bar lines to complete the following rhythms.

4. Match each musical term or sign with the English definition. (Not all definitions will be used.)

Term		Definition	
volta	c	a)	be silent
grandioso	g	b)	soft, subdued, under the breath
mesto	j	c)	time
pesante	h	d)	with fire
tacet	a	e)	playful
sotto voce	b	f)	sonorous
scherzando	e	g)	grand, grandiose
con fuoco	d	h)	weighty, with emphasis
sostenuto	l	i)	with grace
sonore	f	j)	sad, mournful
con grazia	i	k)	with motion
		l)	sustained

__10

5.   a) Name the following intervals.

Aug 5   Maj 3   dim 8   Maj 2   dim 7

b) Change the upper note of each interval enharmonically. Rename the interval.

min 6   dim 4   Maj 7   dim 3   Maj 6

6.   Identify the work to which each of the following statements applies by writing the appropriate letter (A, B, C, D or E) in the space before each statement.

A - Overture to A Midsummer Night's Dream
B - Étude in c minor, opus 10, number 12
10 C - Petrushka, First Tableau: The Crowd Revels at the Shrovetide Fair
D - Dripsody
E - Ko-Ko

a) _E_ This piece is a twelve-bar blues composition with an introduction, 7 choruses and a coda.

b) _B_ This piece is to be performed by a virtuosic solo pianist.

c) _D_ This piece was composed by a Canadian scientist and physicist.

d) _C_ This ballet features polytonality.

e) _E_ This piece is written to be performed by a "big band" type of orchestra.

f) _B_ The nickname for this piece is "Revolutionary".

g) _A_ This piece is an example of 19th Century Program Music.

h) _D_ This piece was created using an eyedropper, a metal wastebasket and a tape recorder.

i) _B_ The tempo of this piece, which features chromatic harmony, is "allegro con fuoco".

j) _C_ This piece is an example of Russian Nationalism and includes Russian subjects, folk music and Russian dances.

7. Match each description in the left column with the correct Triad in the right column.

a) The Supertonic Triad of C Major, in first inversion. — j

10

b) The Dominant Triad of C flat Major, in second inversion. — f

c) The Tonic Triad of G flat Major, in root position. — h

d) The Leading Tone Triad of A flat Major, in first inversion. — a

e) The Mediant Triad of C sharp Major, in root position. — b

f) The Dominant Triad of f sharp minor harmonic form, in second inversion. — i

g) The Submediant Triad of a sharp minor harmonic form, in first inversion. — k

h) The Subdominant Triad of B flat Major in root position. — e

i) The Supertonic Triad of g sharp minor harmonic form, in first inversion. — c

j) The Subdominant Triad of b flat minor harmonic form, in second inversion. — d

k) The Leading Tone Triad of a minor harmonic form, in second inversion. — g

8. Complete the Transposition Chart by adding in either the missing Interval of Transposition (including the direction) or the missing New Key Name for each of the following.

10

Original Key Name	Interval of Transposition	New Key Name
A flat Major	Up a minor 3	Up to Cb Major
c sharp minor	Down an Augmented 4	Down to g minor
d minor	Down a diminished 5	Down to g sharp minor
B Major	Up a diminished 3	Up to D flat Major
B flat Major	Down a Major 7	Down to Cb Major
f minor	Up a Major 6	Up to d minor
d sharp minor	Up a minor 2	Up to e minor
D flat Major	Down a Major 2	Down to C flat Major
E Major	Up a Perfect 5	Up to B Major
a minor	Down an Augmented 4	Down to e flat minor

9. Rewrite the following rhythms beaming the notes correctly.

10

10. Analyze this excerpt from Chopin's Invention No. 9 in f minor by answering the questions below.

Andante con espressione

a) Explain the tempo. <u>moderately slow, with expression</u>
   (walking pace)

b) For the triad at letter **A**, identify: Root: <u>D♭</u>   Quality: <u>Major</u>   Position: <u>1st inv</u>

c) Identify the interval at letter **B**. <u>Min 2</u>.   Identify the interval at letter **C**. <u>Maj 6</u>.

d) For the triad at letter **D**, identify: Root: <u>E</u>   Quality: <u>dim</u>   Position: <u>1st inv</u>

e) Name the notes (letter names) at letter **E**. <u>C</u>   <u>D♮</u>   <u>E♮</u>   <u>F</u>

f) Add the correct rest a letter **F**. Name the type of rest used: <u>Sixteenth</u>

g) Name the notes (letter names) at letter **G**. <u>F</u>   <u>G</u>   <u>A♭</u>   <u>B♭</u>

h) Circle an example of a Whole Step (Whole Tone). Label it as "WS".

i) Circle an example of a Diatonic Half Step (Diatonic Semitone). Label it as "DH".

j) In this excerpt: Identify the number of ties. <u>4</u>   Identify the number of slurs. <u>10</u>

1. Write the following Solid (Blocked) Triads or Chords (in close position). Use a Key Signature and accidentals as needed. Use whole notes.

Key:	E Major	f minor	f# minor	F Major	c minor

Functional Chord Symbol:	vi^6	III+$^6_4$	ii°	IV$^6_4$	V$^4_2$

Root/Quality Chord Symbol:	G#m/B	D7/A	A#°	Gm/D	D#°7

Key:	g# minor	G Major	B Major	E♭ Major	e minor

2. Add Time Signatures to complete the following rhythms.

3. a) Name the key of this melody.
    b) Compose a four-measure Answer phrase to create a **Contrasting** Period. End on a stable scale degree. (There will be more than one correct answer.)
    c) Draw a phrase mark over the Question (Antecedent) phrase and over the contrasting Answer (Consequent) phrase.

___
10
    d) Label the type of cadence (Authentic or Half) at the end of each phrase.

Key: __D♭ Major__   Cadence: __Half__   I   V

Cadence: __Authentic__   V   I

4. Write the definition for each of the following terms.

    a) subito forte   __Suddenly loud__

___
10 b) sotto voce   __Soft, subdued, under the breath__

    c) scherzando   __playful (in a playful manner)__

    d) volti subito   __(v.s.) turn the page quickly__

    e) quindicesima alta   __play the notes under this sign ¹⁵ᵐᵃ two octaves higher__

    f) meno mosso   __less movement, slower__

    g) ad libitum   __(ad lib.) at the liberty of the performer__

    h) rubato   __with some freedom of tempo to enhance musical expression__

    i) martellato   __Strongly accented, hammered__

    j) morendo   __dying, fading away (gradually get softer and slower)__

5.   The following melody is in the key of b flat minor.

   a) Transpose the given melody down a diminished 3rd in the same clef. Use the correct Key
   10 Signature. Name the new key.

Key: _g# minor_

   b) Transpose the given melody up into the key of e minor in the same clef. Use the correct Key
   Signature. Name the interval of transposition.

Interval of Transposition: _Up an Augmented 4_

6.   a) Write the following harmonic interval below each of the given notes. Use whole notes.

   10

   Augmented 2   Perfect 4   Major 7   minor 6   diminished 3

   b) Invert the above intervals in the same clef. Name the inversions.

   dim 7   Per 5   min 2   Maj 3   Aug 6

7. Name the following scales as Major, natural minor, harmonic minor, melodic minor, Whole Tone, Chromatic, Major Pentatonic, minor Pentatonic, Blues or Octatonic.

10 a) __Blues__

b) __minor Pentatonic__

c) __Whole Tone__

d) __Octatonic__

e) __Chromatic__

f) __melodic minor__

g) __Whole Tone__

h) __harmonic minor__

i) __Major__

j) __Major Pentatonic__

8. a) Name the key of the following melody.

Key: f# minor

b) Rewrite the melody at the same pitch. Use a Key Signature and any necessary accidentals.

9. For each of the following:

a) Name the key.
b) Name the type of Cadence (Authentic or Half).

Key: A Major   f minor   G Major

Cadence: Half   Authentic   Half

Key: a♭ minor   C# Major

Cadence: Half   Authentic

10. Analyze this excerpt from Variation II of Mozart's 12 Variations on "Ah, Vous Dirai-Je, Maman" by answering the questions below.

a) Circle a recurrence of the notes (melodic and rhythmic) at letter **A**.

b) Identify the interval at letter **B**. _dim 5_ . Identify the interval at letter **C**. _Maj 3_ .

c) Identify the letter names of the notes at letter **D**. _A_ _G_ _F#_

d) Explain the sign at letter **E**. _breath mark - take a breath and/or a slight pause (or lift - bowed instruments)_

e) This excerpt begins on Measure 57. Add the correct measure number at letter **F**.

f) Identify the interval at letter **G**. _Per 5_ . Identify the interval at letter **H**. _Min 2_ .

g) Explain the sign at letter **I**. _Cresc. becoming louder_

h) For the note at letter **J**, identify: Note Name: _E_ Type of Note: _dotted eighth note_

i) For the note at letter **K**, identify: Note Name: _F_ Type of Note: _sixteenth note_

j) In this excerpt, identify the: Number of Ties: _2_ Number of Slurs: _4_

Total Score: _____
100

1. a) Name the following intervals.

10

Aug 4   dim 8   min 2   Maj 3   dim 5

b) Change the lower note of each interval enharmonically. Rename the interval.

dim 5   Maj 7   Aug 1   dim 4   Aug 4

2. a) Name the key.
   b) Write a Cadence in Keyboard Style below the bracketed notes.
   c) Label the chords using Functional Chord Symbols.
   d) Name the type of Cadence (Authentic or Half).

10

Key: Eb Major   I   V   V   I

Cadence: _____ Half _____   Cadence: _____ Authentic _____

Key: d# minor   i   V   V   i

(*also correct iv – V)

Cadence: _____ Half _____   Cadence: _____ Authentic _____

3. Match each description in the left column with the correct Chord or Triad in the right column.

a) The Supertonic Triad of e minor natural form, in first inversion. — K

10

b) The Subdominant Triad of f minor harmonic form, in second inversion. — e

c) The Leading Tone Triad of d sharp minor harmonic form, in root position. — b

d) The Dominant Seventh Chord of G flat Major, in third inversion. — a

e) The Submediant Triad of F sharp Major, in second inversion. — g

f) The Leading Tone Diminished Seventh Chord of d minor, in root position. — i

g) The Tonic Triad of D flat Major, in first inversion. — c

h) The Mediant Triad of b flat minor harmonic form, in root position. — h

i) The Dominant Seventh Chord of b minor harmonic form, in second inversion. — f

j) The Dominant Triad of a flat minor harmonic form, in first inversion. — d

k) The Supertonic Triad of c sharp minor harmonic form, in second inversion. — j

4. For each of the following Seventh Chords:

    a) Name the key.
    b) Name the type of Chord.

Key: G Major   a minor   g minor   b minor   E♭ Major

Chord: Dom 7th   Dom 7th   dim 7th   dim 7th   Dom 7th

5. Fill in the blanks for any ten (10) of the following. (All answers provided)

    a) Identify the key of Chopin's "Revolutionary Etude". __C minor__

    b) Identify the Composer of "Dripsody". __Hugh Le Caine__

    c) Identify a Polytonal Ballet by Stravinsky. __Petrushka__

    d) Identify the Composer of "Overture to a Midsummer Night's Dream". __Mendelssohn__

    e) Identify the Era from around 1825 to 1900. __Romantic Era__

    f) Identify the Era from around the 1900 to the current date. __Modern Era__

    g) Identify the Genre of "Ko-Ko". __Jazz (Big Band)__

    h) Identify the type of chord made famous by Stravinsky. __Petrushka Chord (polychord)__

    i) Identify the Composer of "Ko-Ko". __Duke Ellington__

    j) Identify the Performing Forces for "Ko-Ko". __Big Band Orchestra__

    k) Identify the Genre of "Dripsody". __electronic music__

    l) Identify the Performing Forces for the "Revolutionary Etude". __piano__

6.   Identify and explain the following signs.

___
10

a) 〜 _glissando - continuous slide_
upward between 2 or more pitches

b) 15ma⌐ _quindicesima alta - play the notes_
under the sign two octaves higher

c) ⊓ _down bow - on a bowed string instrument,_
play the note while drawing the bow downward

d) , _breath mark - take a breath, and/or a_
slight pause or lift

e) V _up bow - on a bowed string instrument,_
play the note while drawing the bow upward

7.   For the following melody:

a) Name the key.
b) Above the staff, write the Root/Quality Chord Symbol (in root position) outlined by the notes
___ in each measure.
10
c) Below the staff, write the Functional Chord Symbol (in root position) outlined by the notes in
    each measure.
d) Circle and label any passing tones as pt. Circle and label any neighbor tones as nt.

Root/Quality
Chord Symbol: **G m**   **C m**   **D**   **G m**

Key: _g minor_

Functional
Chord Symbol: _i_   _iv_   _V_   _i_

Ultimate Music Theory
LEVEL 7 Supplemental Exam #7

8. Add rests below the brackets to complete each of the following measures.

9. Identify the Major or minor key for each of the following.

a) The Tonic minor key of F sharp Major. $f\sharp$ minor

10. b) The Enharmonic Relative minor key of C sharp Major. $b\flat$ minor

c) The Major key with B as the Dominant note.   E Major

d) The Enharmonic Tonic Major key of b minor. $C\flat$ Major

e) The Relative Major key of e flat minor. $G\flat$ Major

f) The minor key with E flat as the Subtonic.   f minor

g) The Enharmonic Tonic minor key of G flat Major. $f\sharp$ minor

h) The minor key with G Double Sharp as the Leading Tone. $a\sharp$ minor

i) The Major key with C as the Supertonic. $B\flat$ Major

j) The Tonic Major key of b flat minor. $B\flat$ Major

10.   Analyze this excerpt from *Sly Snake* by Julianne Warkentin by answering the questions below.

a) Write the Time Signature directly on the music.

b) Explain the tempo mark. _Very slow with expression_

c) Circle a recurrence of the notes (melodic and rhythmic) at letter **A**.

d) Add the rest at letter **B**. Identify the type of rest used. _dotted quarter rest_

e) Explain the sign at letter **C**. _Play one octave above the written pitch_

f) Explain the sign at letter **D**. _Treble Clef indicates change to Treble Clef_

g) This excerpt begins on Measure 1. Add the correct measure number at letter **E**.

h) Identify the interval at letter **F**. _dim 3_ . Identify the interval at letter **G**. _Maj 3_ .

i) Explain the sign at letter **H**. _pedal marking - use damper pedal (on the piano)_

j) Identify the letter names of the notes at letter **I**. _F#_   _Ab_   _C_

Ultimate Music Theory
LEVEL 7 Supplemental Exam #8

Total Score: _____
100

1. a) Name the following intervals.

Maj 2   Maj 3   min 6   dim 4

b) Change the lower note of each interval enharmonically. Rename the interval.

dim 3   dim 4   Aug 5   Maj 3

c) Write the following harmonic interval below each of the given notes. Use whole notes.

Perfect 5   Augmented 3   minor 6   diminished 7

d) Invert the above intervals in the same clef. Name the inversions.

Per 4   dim 6   Maj 3   Aug 2

e) Write the following melodic interval above each of the given notes. Use half notes.

Major 6   Perfect 4   minor 2   Augmented 7

Ultimate Music Theory
LEVEL 7 Supplemental Exam #8

2.   a) Add rests below the brackets to complete each of the following measures.

b) Add Time Signatures to complete the following rhythms.

c) Add bar lines to complete each of the following rhythms.

Ultimate Music Theory
LEVEL 7 Supplemental Exam #8

3.   Write the following scales, ascending and descending. Use whole notes.

   a) The Chromatic scale starting on A. Use a Key Signature. Use any standard notation.

<u>10</u>

   b) The Whole Tone scale starting on D sharp. Use accidentals.

   c) The Major Pentatonic scale starting on E flat. Use a Key Signature.

   d) The Blues scale starting on A. Use accidentals. Use any standard notation.

(also correct A C D D# E G A)

   e) The minor Pentatonic scale starting on B. Use accidentals.

4.   a) The following melody is in the key of A Major. Transpose the given melody down an
         Augmented 4th in the same clef. Use the correct Key Signature. Name the new key.

Key: __Eb Major__

   b) Transpose the given melody up into the key of B Major in the same clef. Name the
       interval of transposition.

Interval of Transposition: ___Up a Major 2___

   c) Name the key of the following melody.

Key: ___g# minor___

   d) Rewrite the melody at the same pitch. Use a Key Signature and any necessary accidentals.

5. a) Write the following Solid (Blocked) Chords in the Treble Clef using a Key Signature and any necessary accidentals. Use whole notes. Write the Root/Quality Chord Symbol above and the Functional Chord Symbol below.

10 i) The Dominant Seventh Chord of E Major in second inversion.
   ii) The Supertonic Triad of g minor harmonic form in first inversion.
   iii) The Leading Tone Triad of D Major in root position.
   iv) The Dominant Triad of c sharp minor harmonic form in second inversion.
   v) The Leading-Tone Diminished Seventh Chord of d minor in root position.

Root/Quality
Chord Symbol: i) $B^7/F\#$ ii) A°/C iii) $C\#^\circ$ iv) $G\#/D\#$ v) $C\#^{\circ7}$

Functional
Chord Symbol: i) V^4_3 ii) $ii^{\circ6}_3$ iii) vii° iv) V^6_4 v) $vii^{\circ7}$

b) For each of the following Seventh Chords, name the key. Write the Root/Quality Chord Symbol above each Chord. Write the Functional Chord Symbol below each Chord.

Root/Quality
Chord Symbol: $G\#^{\circ7}$ $A^7/C\#$ $A\#^7/E\#$ B^{b7} F^7/E^b

Key: a minor   D Major   d# minor   e♭ minor   B♭ Major

Functional
Chord Symbol: $vii^{\circ7}$ V^6_5 V^4_3 V^7 V^4_2

6. a) Name the key.
   b) Write a Cadence in Keyboard Style below the bracketed notes.
   c) Label the chords using Functional Chord Symbols.
   d) Name the type of Cadence (Authentic or Half).

Key: D Major

(Also correct IV - V)

I   V   V   I

Cadence: Half   Cadence: Authentic

Key: f minor   i   V   V   i

Cadence: Half   Cadence: Authentic

d) For each of the following, name the key. Name the type of Cadence (Authentic or Half).

Key: e minor   F Major   g minor   C Major

Cadence: Half   Half   Authentic   Half

7. For the following melody:

   i) Name the key of this melody.
   ii) Compose a four-measure Answer phrase to create a **Contrasting** Period. End on a stable scale degree. (There will be more than one correct answer.)

   ___
   10 iii) Draw a phrase mark over the Question (Antecedent) phrase and over the contrasting Answer (Consequent) phrase.
   iv) Label the type of cadence (Authentic or Half) at the end of each phrase.

Key: **B♭ Major**

Cadence: **Half**

(one possible answer)

Cadence: **Authentic**

b) For the following melody:

   i) Name the key.
   ii) Above the staff, write the Root/Quality Chord Symbol (in root position) outlined by the notes in each measure.
   iii) Below the staff, write the Functional Chord Symbol (in root position) outlined by the notes in each measure.
   iv) Circle and label any passing tones as pt. Circle and label any neighbor tones as nt.

Root/Quality
Chord Symbol: **A♯m**   **D♯m**   **E**   **A♯m**

Key: **a♯ minor**

Functional
Chord Symbol: **i**   **iv**   **V**   **i**

8. For each of the following terms and signs, circle whether the definition is True or False.

a) TRUE or ~~FALSE~~ *sotto voce*   -   return to the original speed

10 b) ~~TRUE~~ or FALSE: *dolente*   -   sad

c) TRUE or ~~FALSE:~~ *15ma*   -   play one octave higher

d) TRUE or ~~FALSE~~ *agitato*   -   moderately slow, at a walking pace

e) ~~TRUE~~ or FALSE: *tacet*   -   be silent

f) ~~TRUE~~ or FALSE: *giocoso*   -   humorous, jocose

g) ~~TRUE~~ or FALSE: *martellato*   -   strongly accented, hammered

h) TRUE or ~~FALSE~~ V   -   play the note while drawing the bow downward

i) TRUE or ~~FALSE:~~ *pesante*   -   expressive, with expression

j) ~~TRUE~~ or FALSE: 〰〰   -   continuous slide upward or downward between pitches

k) ~~TRUE~~ or FALSE: *morendo*   -   dying, fading away

l) ~~TRUE~~ or FALSE: *grandioso*   -   grand, grandiose

m) TRUE or ~~FALSE~~ *semplice*   -   continue in the same manner as has just been played

n) ~~TRUE~~ or FALSE: *sopra*   -   above

o) TRUE or ~~FALSE~~ *vivo*   -   sweet, gentle

p) ~~TRUE~~ or FALSE: *sostenuto*   -   sustained

q) TRUE or ~~FALSE~~ *mesto*   -   marked or stressed

r) TRUE or ~~FALSE~~ *risoluto*   -   with some freedom of tempo to enhance expression

s) ~~TRUE~~ or FALSE: *scherzando*   -   playful, playfully

t) ~~TRUE~~ or FALSE: *tutti*   -   a passage for the ensemble

9. Identify the work or the Composer to which each of the following statements applies by placing the appropriate letter in the space provided.

__10__

A - Petrushka
B - Etude in c minor, opus 10, number 12
C - Overture to A Midsummer Night's Dream
D - Dripsody
E - Ko-Ko

F - Felix Mendelssohn
G - Duke Ellington
H - Igor Stravinsky
I - Hugh Le Caine
J - Frédéric Chopin

a) **G** - This Grammy Award Winning American Composer was also a pianist.

b) **B** - This piano piece was nicknamed "Revolutionary".

c) **H** - This Russian Modern Era Composer called himself an "Inventor of Music".

d) **I** - This 20th-Century Canadian Composer was also a Scientist and Physicist.

e) **E** - This jazz piece is in 12-Bar Blues Form and is performed by an orchestra.

f) **J** - This "Poet of the Piano" was born in Poland in the Romantic Era.

g) **A** - This ballet in Rondo Form features polytonality and Pentatonic scales.

h) **C** - This piece of Program Music was inspired by a play by Shakespeare.

i) **D** - This electronic music was created from the recording of a single drop of water.

j) **F** - This German Composer and his sister Fanny wrote music in the Romantic Era.

k) **G** - This Composer played a major role in the development of the Big-Band Era.

l) **A** - This piece features a Polychord - two dissonant chords clashing together.

m) **A** - This piece tells the story of 3 puppets brought to life by a "Magician".

n) **E** - This piece in e flat minor features an Introduction, 7 Choruses and a Coda.

o) **C** - This piece is written in Sonata form (3 distinct sections) in the key of E Major.

p) **J** - This Composer often used "rubato", a free flowing flexible rhythmic tempo.

q) **I** - This Composer created 22 new electronic musical instruments.

r) **C** - This piece is introduced by 4 "Magic Chords" played by Woodwinds and Brass.

s) **H** - This Composer was inducted into the Hollywood Walk of Fame in 1960.

t) **I** - This Composer invented the "Multi-Track", a Special Purpose Tape Recorder.

10. Analyze this excerpt from *Swingin' Squirrel* by Julianne Warkentin by answering the questions below.

a) At letter **A**, add a dynamic sign to play very loud.

b) Circle a recurrence of the notes (melodic and rhythmic) at letter **B**.

c) For the triad at letter **C**, identify: Root: _A_ Quality: _minor_ Position: _2nd inv_

d) For the triad at letter **D**, identify: Root: _A_ Quality: _dim_ Position: _2nd inv_

e) Add the rest at letter **E**. Identify the type of rest used. _eighth rest_

f) Add the rest at letter **F**. Identify the type of rest used. _half rest_

g) This excerpt begins on Measure 13. Add the missing Measure Number at letter **G**.

h) Identify the type of scale at letter **H**. _chromatic_

i) Explain the sign at letter **I**. _triplet - 3 notes played in the time of 2 notes of the same value_

j) Explain the sign at letter **J**. _ottava, play one octave above written pitch_

TOP 10 Ultimate Music Theory Tips
To Score 100% on Exams

Tip #1: Students should complete at least 8 Practice Examinations before writing their Final Exam. LEVEL 7 Exams will have two hours to be completed.

Tip #2: Hold a "Practice Examination" in your studio. Have all students who are writing their Exams come at the same time. They can only bring a ruler, eraser and pencil. Set a Timer. When the timer starts, the examination begins – no talking, no cell phones, no open books!

Tip #3: Pizza Party! On the night before their Examinations, have a "Pizza Party" – Use the Ultimate Music Theory Flashcards App, UMT Whiteboard and UMT Games to review terminology and concepts. Everyone will have fun and everything will be fresh in their minds.

Tip #4: On Exam day, Students should arrive 15 minutes before the start time of their Examination.

Tip #5: If the Student is not given a piece of blank paper to use to write out their UMT Map before beginning their Examination, they should ask for one from the Exam Center Representative. (Have your Student practice asking for a blank piece of paper.)

Tip #6: Remind both Student and Parent that it is the Student's responsibility to bring a mechanical pencil (with extra lead), or 2 - 3 pencils (with a pencil sharpener), eraser and ruler. They cannot bring any items that have "music" on them, so they cannot bring their UMT Rulers.

Tip #7: It is always a good idea to bring a tissue or two, a bottle of water and a couple of hard candies if it is cold/allergy time. Be sure to get plenty of rest the day before the exam.

Tip #8: Complete the exam in order beginning with question 1. Review what your Student can do if they get stuck – if their brain goes blank on a question. One suggestion would be to continue to the next question and then go back later to finish that question.

Tip #9: Remind Students to look at the front AND back of each page to ensure that ALL questions have been answered… and checked… and double checked.

Tip #10: Ultimate Music Theory 100% Club - *The Way to Score Success!* You and your student can become a member of the UMT 100% Club when your student receives a score of 100% on their nationally recognized theory exams including the RCM Theory Examinations.

Go to UltimateMusicTheory.com and complete the UMT 100% Club Form
to receive your special 100% Club Certificate & Congratulations!

Workbooks, Exams, Answers, Online Courses, App & More!

A Proven Step-by-Step System to Learn Theory Faster - from Beginner to Advanced.

Innovative techniques designed to develop a complete understanding of music theory, to enhance sight reading, ear training, creativity, composition and musical expression.

All UMT Series have matching Answer Books!

The UMT Rudiments Series - Beginner A, Beginner B, Beginner C, Prep 1, Prep 2, Basic, Intermediate, Advanced & Complete (All-In-One)

♪ 12 Lessons, Review Tests, and a Final Exam to develop confidence
♪ Music Theory Guide & Chart for fast and easy reference of theory concepts
♪ 80 Flashcards for fun drills to dramatically increase retention & comprehension

Rudiments Exam Series - Preparatory, Basic, Intermediate & Advanced

♪ 8 Exams plus UMT Tips on How to Score 100% on Theory Exams

Each Rudiments Workbook correlates to a Supplemental Workbook.

The UMT Supplemental Series - Prep Level, Level 1, Level 2, Level 3, Level 4, Level 5, Level 6, Level 7, Level 8 & Complete (All-In-One) Level

♪ Form & Analysis and Music History - Composers, Eras & Musical Styles
♪ Melody Writing using ICE - Imagine, Compose & Explore
♪ 12 Lessons, Review Tests, Final Exam and 80 Flashcards for quick study

Supplemental Exam Series - Level 5, Level 6, Level 7 & Level 8

♪ 8 Exams to successfully prepare for nationally recognized Theory Exams

UMT Online Courses, Music Theory App & More

♪ UMT Certification Course, Teachers Membership & Elite Educator Program
♪ Ultimate Music Theory App correlates to the Rudiments Workbooks
♪ Free Resources - Teachers Guide, Music Theory Blogs, videos & downloads

Go To: **UltimateMusicTheory.com**